Mary Coll

SILVER

with images by Margaret Lonergan

ARLEN
HOUSE

Silver

is published in 2017 by

ARLEN HOUSE
42 Grange Abbey Road
Baldoyle, Dublin 13, Ireland
Phone: 00 353 86 8207617
arlenhouse@gmail.com
arlenhouse.blogspot.com

Distributed internationally by
SYRACUSE UNIVERSITY PRESS
621 Skytop Road, Suite 110
Syracuse, NY 13244–5290
Phone: 315–443–5534
Fax: 315–443–5545
supress@syr.edu
syracuseuniversitypress.syr.edu

ISBN 978–1–85132–163–6, paperback

LIMERICK
arts
OFFICE

Supported by Limerick Arts Office, Limerick City and County
Council, and the Arts Council

SILVER

CONTENTS

For John, Ellen, Katherine, and Joan
with love

SILVER

SILVER

How far can I go with this before I scare you?
I'd better not say that you are all my joy, all of it,
you'd find that too ridiculous, and laugh,
or that I still watch you sleeping, sometimes,
because that's just too weird.
I won't mention how hard I fight the urge
to hold you back
almost every time you go to leave,
for school, or the cinema, or walk the dog,
only almost, though,
I mean I'm not that crazy, really.
I know you'll come back later,
later than we agreed, always,
but then what if you don't,
where would I take myself then?
Maybe that empty car park on the outskirts
of madness where nobody hears me banging
my head on the horn, over and over,
because my throat is too raw from howling,
and there are no tears left,
not even the dust of a tear in the duct of my eye,
refusing to silence my grief.
Who would do that, you ask, horrified,
strolling away from the table,
trailing crumbs in your wake.
Me, I don't say, to your immense relief,
reminding you instead to put the lid on the jam
and call me, please,
because you are the star attraction in the circus
I never ran away to,
spinning effortlessly without a net,
while I watch, with one eye closed in terror, the other wide
open in amazement, seeing you sparkle like silver,
terrified you'll catch your death of cold in that costume.

NEW YEAR

You can't wait to get started,
to be up to your neck in July,
everything swept away by your new resolve,
the wheat and sugar, the dairy and salt,
your father's ghost tapping on your shoulder
until the cupboards are bare.
There is talk of the Camino,
maps are dragged out, Machu Picchu is found,
you can walk there too, and Uluru,
always Uluru, that road not taken,
until the world becomes your oyster again,
because oysters are always good.
I lack your appetite for change.
It is better to stay out of sight of the gods,
arguing over where the decorations go,
putting the lights away carefully,
hoping to be around when they're taken back out again.
Our greatest challenge for the year ahead,
to remain as we are,
in the half light of a January day,
imperfect and complete.

HUNGRY HEART

It's been on the radio all week,
our song, the one from that vinyl we scratched
when our feet stumbled in the dark
and we found each other the first time.
The one I kept, the one you thought was taken
by a Second Year from Donegal who crashed
on your sofa that long weekend.
Years have gone by almost without
a second thought of you.
Still, in those opening bars, it's always your voice I hear,
at the end of that J1 summer, fresh from your pilgrimage
to Asbury Park, a slight twang to your lyrics,
all your new-found New Jersey bluff and bluster
turning my head,
making me forgive and forget,
while the saxophone riff drowns out
your already broken promises.

OMENS

The daffodils have come too soon,
they unsettle me, sitting in the living room
like guests who got their dates wrong.
The omens are not good,
the neighbour's cat has disappeared,
not necessarily a bad thing,
there was a robin at the window yesterday,
a sign of death, or is it money,
in the suburbs the entrails are hard to read.
Everything is the same, inside and out.
At school, global warming is the new religion,
its most eager converts rummage through
our dustbin for evidence of heresy.
Everything is now my fault, even the weather.
A pair of swans fly low, perfect as a painting,
silent as the air itself they move against the evening sky
over heads bent sorting the cardboard from the glass.

This is not the West Village,
finding excitement here requires skill.
It takes patience to establish where the fox has her lair,
which house the Jack Russell belongs to,
where the ginger cat considers home.
Herons squall in the high trees at the intersection,
making an African dawn easier to imagine
– imagination being essential to all of this.
It allows you to explain the different car every morning
outside the house named after a small town in Texas,
the tall man with the kind eyes smoking
his first cigarette of the day
with only garden gnomes for company,
the sad woman with the pink gloves
at the bus stop every morning
who speaks no English, or chooses not to,
the skinny boy leaving far too early for school.
These are my neighbours,
the strangers I will be found beside if the sky falls.
Whatever it is we are in, we are in it together,
here among these parks, lawns and groves,
shaped by a burning desire to make everything the same.
Our triumphs are small ones;
the colour of paint on a gable wall,
a driveway paved with three shades of brick,
the flash of a gleaming Harley under tarpaulin,
a camper van with blue gingham curtains
always ready for the road.

Truth

Cross my heart and hope to die.
That's the second lie I told you,
which means you now know the first.
What can I say?
Be careful what you wish for.
In the end it was only a tiny grain
shaved from the full truth,
from which I spared you,
just enough to keep you on your toes,
small as a pebble in your shoe,
a sliver of timber buried in the palm of your hand,
a paper cut to your tender skin,
you embraced it like a martyr's cilice,
ecstatic in your pain,
radiant in your agony,
praying that above all else your wound might never heal.

PATMOS

Years later, on yet another ferry,
while the rest were out of earshot,
out of the blue you asked what I remembered.
Did I remember the elephant in that room
too small to swing a cat?
What happened, in those few moments
when everything that happened next,
might never have happened at all.
The surprise of your lips on mine,
the salt taste of your warm summer skin,
being wide awake as I walked away,
terrified I might run back.
No point telling you, really,
when that was all I could remember,
along with a place where they sold fish,
it was in all the photographs,
though where they are now is anyone's guess.

Mini Break

It's called a mini break,
this sugar rush of time that makes my head spin
in a hotel with more stars than the Milky Way,
an all-we-can't-eat breakfast,
a spa where they wrap you in chocolate, out of spite.
There are even kites to fly on the beach,
and time,
me time,
down time,
time out,
time to do whatever we want,
free and unlimited, like the wifi.
Finally, our time,
all the time in the world,
stretching out before us now like a threat.

RINGS

The ring you lost was one of a pair
we bought for cash on the cheap
from a travelling salesman,
the friend of a friend.
That night in her garden,
just days before we were married,
he placed a dark velvet tray on the white plastic table
and asked us to choose.
Back then all rings looked the same to us,
you thought a ring was just a ring,
and so did I,
knowing nothing and everything as we did,
with no idea what the real price would be,
what each of us would pay,
what those rings would see and hear,
where we would take them together,
where we would take them alone.
The ring you lost was one of a kind,
something we both learned the hard way.

MIDPOINT

We walked the length of the East Pier
and back in silence,
before that we swam silently among
the early morning regulars at Seapoint.
Later we will sit on the rocks in the sunshine
letting our thoughts freefall without a sound.
We are at a point where it is no longer
always necessary to speak.
I have told you almost everything there is to tell,
it's enough now for us just to be together,
wordlessly passing sections
of the newspaper back and forth,
knowing when it is time to put the kettle on,
not having to ask about milk or sugar,
red or white, or anything.
This is the part where I can hear
you breathe without listening
and you remember the dreams
I have forgotten on waking.

FAIRY TALE

Long after happy ever after, you're still waiting
to be swept off your feet.
It's a lot to expect, even in fairyland
where tomorrow never comes.
Here we are again, trying to figure it all out
while the coffee goes cold.
You forgot that a girl can't run far in glass slippers,
you forgot you had dreams even bigger than mine,
a lifetime ago you read them out loud to me
from the clouds over our heads,
back when the possibilities were endless,
when there was no stopping you,
when there was nothing you wouldn't try once.
The second time I should have tried harder.
Once upon a time I thought you could slay dragons,
but you're even more afraid of the dark than me,
the eldest child left to turn out all the lights
and feel her way back.
Time to turn them on again,
to listen carefully.
There is no Prince Charming.
You make your own wishes come true,
the ending is still all yours to re-write.

LAUNDRY

My grandfather sent everything to the nuns
for a thorough cleaning,
including my mother.
Fervently they washed every stain away,
held us up to the light
so there's hardly a trace of me left in her
or her left in me.
Things are forever getting separated in the wash,
a fawn silk stocking,
a tiny pink sock with no matcher,
the price to be paid for getting your laundry done.

LANDSCAPE

The day is perfect, infinite blue sea and sky
barely separated by yellow, gorse-covered mountains,
all of nature just thrilled with the wonder of itself,
the kind of day you dream of, when dreams can be
squandered on scenery, not held tightly in your fist
knowing you have maybe one or two left,
and everyone wants a little,
everyone except you.
There is nothing I can give you now, not even a dream.
Here where I watch the waves fizzle out along the shore
I taught you to walk, and later to swim,
here is where you chased seagulls
and threw jellyfish at the moon.
On a bad line from another world
your voice tells me you are barely able to crawl.
There is nothing I can do
but watch swans move effortlessly
across a chocolate box lake,
holding my breath, while my feet on the wet sand
feel the whole world turn beneath them.

JUST DESSERTS

In a café around the corner from where Marie Antoinette
lost her head,
you also lose yours over a cake.
At home, you inform me, we could have three
for the price of a slice here.
But we are not at home now, dear,
we are in Paris,
or at least one of us is,
besides, who needs three cakes anyway.
You flick through the guidebook, eager
to narrate us on our way again,
determined not to miss a trick, but then you do.
At the next table the man in the pale grey suit
with the mauve silk tie
lifts a forkful of impeccable pastry towards the lips
of a girl half his age,
his hand perfectly poised before them
and they open to him, for the umpteenth time that day,
while he smiles the smile
of one who knows the real
pleasure of having his cake and eating it.

We are hopelessly lost on the deserted streets
of an Algarve town.
In blistering heat the hotel where we
honeymooned a lifetime ago
refuses to be found,
a place not worth discovering the first time,
though it mattered little to us then,
coming on it late at night,
confetti stuck to the soles of our shoes,
your face mutinous under the strain
of my two large suitcases,
my eyes unable to hide the feeling
that maybe it was all some terrible mistake.
Our adult children are vaguely amused;
it's the most we can hope from them these days.
You insist it was closer to the square,
I remember a fountain, and blue shutters on the windows,
you are certain there were no shutters, and no fountain,
but there was a bar next door, on that we both agree.
They played the Gypsy Kings all night,
making it impossible to sleep,
not that we slept much, you say, and I laugh,
and our adult children are less amused.
Settled finally at a table near the harbour,
having recognised nothing,
you briefly cover my hand with yours,
winking as you pass the bread,
and our precise whereabouts, as always,
become immaterial.

Moving Out

You said he loved you and that you loved him,
as if that was all there was to say.
So I held my tongue all summer until it got too heavy.
Then a week before you left I made my salad,
without the olives.
Two days later I made my apple tart, without the cloves.
Your last night at home, after the car was packed and the
house was finally quiet, I added an extra quilt,
stuffing it in as if my life depended on it, or yours.
Sometimes that is all a mother can do
– leave things out, or add things in,
hoping through a sequence of tiny gestures
to tell the whole story.
One thing I never said is that neither of us
are ready for this goodbye,
though only one of us sees it now.
By the time the other figures it out, winter will have come,
at which point, an extra quilt will be essential.

Parade

The last thing he asked me
was to take him to the parade,
a child's sense of wonder still in his eyes,
and like a child I distracted him,
thinking there would be time,
another time,
not just three sleeps,
four short days,
and then he'd be gone.
That St Patrick's Day he was already marching
to the sound of a different drum,
rounding a final corner,
his memory forever tangled in the traces
of a distant piper's 'Minstrel Boy', carried on an icy breeze
through the grey March streets of our home town.

PLASSEY

Somehow we wound up in Plassey, and I told you
that on summer days like this, it had been the furthest
reaches of my urban child's imagination,
the Elysian Fields, complete with rocks
for jumping off into the treacle river.
Fields and rivers and trees and rocks
do nothing for you, they are things
a country boy goes through,
and across, and around
on his way to someplace better,
the someplace you always want to be.
And grass is for cattle and sheep, not for sitting on,
although in the end you humour me.
So there we are, like that sepia picture on my mother's
wall of the man with the moustache and straw boater,
his wife beside him looking more than a little out of sorts,
having flown the coup for Manhattan, only to fall
for the one man there who would bring her back,
just yards from here, to pose,
on another summer's day like this,
their whole story, like ours,
caught in a moment.
Are we staying long, you ask?
I'm thinking forever, I reply, as you roll
your eyes and sigh to the passing swans.

SIDES

We have taken sides,
mine with the hand cream, the books, the newspapers,
an everest of good intentions,
yours – monastic, just your watch and the radio,
a man who could disappear without a trace.
Occasionally we still meet in the middle,
that common ground first occupied by one child,
then another, sometimes both,
the ebb and flow of their lives
pushing us to opposite shores
though we struggled against it then,
your foot touching mine,
the tip of my fingers brushing the back of your neck,
a semaphore that told us all we needed to know.
I have no memory of us taking sides,
yet here we are,
you with one pillow,
me with three,
all the space in the world between us now
as we exhale this day into the gathering darkness.

SOUNDS

The sound of a friendship ending is similar
to that of a tree falling in the middle of a forest,
and likewise depends on who's listening.
For me, it was like a penny dropping,
what you may have heard, if anything,
is anyone's guess.
Either way, at least it broke the silence of a note
sustained longer than our voices could carry it,
our hearts having given up on the melody ages ago.

TUESDAY EVENING

It is possible for a woman of a certain age
to walk into a room
and, finding a man of a certain age sleeping on the sofa,
stop in her tracks while the negative of the boy she loved
to the point of distraction floats before her.
In that instant, before she boils water for pasta, she runs
over what years of the tide going in and out has left her,
the flotsam and jetsam salvaged from the storms,
what it was like before time took everything
that wasn't tied down,
evenings that came and went, just like this one,
where snow fell, or nothing at all happened,
and nothing of importance was said,
what she has wagered, won and lost,
what she has held back and what she has held on to,
the memory of a girl who could not breathe
unless it was the same air he was breathing,
love's tiny traces,
the hunger for a royal flush that keeps her at the table.

UNCLE

You carried my photo in your wallet
until it fell to pieces in your hands,
hands that wrote to her every week
with news from a place where nothing happened
and nothing was said.
Farmer's hands, big as the page,
shaking as you tell me how she loved to dance,
was the first to sing at parties,
until all the dancing and singing stopped.
It was the way, you said,
hoping more words might come to you
from the pattern of the hotel lobby carpet,
a family of strangers squashed
between a hen party and a funeral,
my husband and your wife
not sure what to do with themselves,
me looking at oarsmen on the river outside,
able to hear only half of what you were saying,
you trying desperately to match my face
with the one you had been keeping in your heart.

WORDS

This might be the poem you're looking for.
Remember how I needed a raft of words
to save myself from you,
words to cling onto,
words to whisper.
Remember when there were never enough words.
Well that was then.
Now you have nothing to fear from my words,
they are the lexicon of a shopping list,
the instruction manual for assembling a desk,
anyone could use them, even you.
You and I have no further use of words.
Left to our own devices we would opt
for a good night's sleep,
our backs are not what they used to be,
neither are our hearts.
Nothing is what it used to be.
This is exactly the poem you're looking for.

I will neglect to mention that I missed you,
and left the curtains open to sleep
under the same blanket of stars,
stars you are as unlikely to have noticed
as you are likely to mention missing me.
I still drive past our old house just to see
how the cherry tree's doing,
the one we planted at the end of our first year
for better or worse.
Our ghosts will linger in its shade,
that much I'm certain of,
remembering a time when all we had
were two stools to fall between.
In the meantime I will clear out a wardrobe,
or write a poem.
It's a way of putting down time,
which is all I do in your absence,
though I will neglect to mention that too,
as we fold back into each other,
neither asking or wanting for anything more.

HEATWAVE

A glimpse of sun teases like the flash
of a burlesque dancer's thigh,
one by one the sky sheds its clouds, until
out of the blue summer stands pouting before me.
I have no idea where to look,
there is a sudden urgency to move, to make the most of it.
Soon the son I never had is mowing the lawn.
Even from a distance you can tell he's
the image of his father.
That's what it does to you,
a sudden change in the weather,
makes you imagine all sorts of things,
shines a light so bright you can see
all the cobwebs and dust,
the grey streaks on the windows,
the lack of adequate garden furniture,
the rust on the barbeque,
the cracks in your marriage.
Everything that winter kept under wraps
is thrown out of synch.
From next door's patio the opening
exchanges of a row rises
before the perfect couple bundle
each other back inside,
then there is only canned laughter
from their television, or is it ours?
On the far side of the back fence,
a carnival of teenagers gathers.
Long into the night they call to each other
across the wide open spaces of youth,
their voices full of longing,
while we lie awake
cursing the heat and dreaming of rain.

GARDEN

What grows here does so in spite of me,
the roses that make it through
the laurel hedge every summer,
the parsley that refuses to give up.
Why you gave me cuttings is beyond me,
Blue Lobelia and Sleeping Shamrock from your rockery.
Put them anywhere and they will thrive, you assured me,
promising I would always have them,
the rest of that sentence left unsaid.
We no longer refer to time,
there is more glass than sand,
things are more easily done than said,
like planting your forget-me-nots
of Blue Lobelia and Sleeping Shamrock,
knowing, that in the absence of faith,
I will need each gentle reminder of love.

ACKNOWLEDGEMENTS

Earlier versions of some of these poems were first published in *Salmon: A Journey in Poetry: New and Selected Poems, 1981– 2007*, edited by Jessie Lendennie (Salmon Poetry, 2007); *Dream of A City: An Anthology of Contemporary Poetry from Limerick City of Culture* (Astrolabe Press, 2014) and *Even The Daybreak: 35 Years of Salmon Poetry* (Salmon Poetry, 2016).

My friend Gabriel Rosenstock uses the word 'transcreation' in place of 'translation'. It comes from a phrase that he found in a volume of Indian poetry: 'transcreated from the Urdu'. I asked to borrow it from him for this statement because 'transcreation' seems to best capture the alchemy that happens when a visual artist responds to a poet's words. The words come first, and then the images, but after that the two art forms enter into a dialogue with each other that goes beyond the original intentions or control of either practitioner. The conversation is between the forms, not between the individuals. Mary and I didn't engage on this project discursively or analytically. We know each other's work, and when Mary envisioned *Silver* as a relationship between word and image, she invited me to respond to the collection. I loved *Silver*, spent time with it, and then through a gently-held interspersion and osmosis, these images gradually found their way towards Mary's words. Roughly three quarters of the images here were created in direct response to *Silver*, and the other quarter were pre-existing images that had been waiting for their true home. In my experience, transcreation seems to be dependant upon a loving, open and sensual attention to the original source from which the words came; entering into this kind of relationship with Mary's work has been a tender privilege.

– Margaret Lonergan

MARY COLL is a poet, playwright and broadcaster from Limerick. The first female editor of *The Stony Thursday Book*, her publications include *All Things Considered* (Salmon, 2002) and, as editor, *Faithful Companions* (Mellick Press, 2009). She has published essays in *Chasing Rainbows* (2002), *The Quiet Quarter* (2004 and 2009) and *Sunday Miscellany* (2006 and 2011). She has made numerous contributions to arts and culture programmes on RTÉ Radio One, RTÉ Lyric FM, and RTÉ Televsion, and has worked as a critic for *The Irish Independent* and other national newspapers. Stage productions of *Excess Baggage* (2007) and *Anything But Love* (2010) were produced at The Belltable Arts Centre. Other work includes radio plays commissioned by RTÉ Drama on One, lyrics for the Choral Work 'Spirestone' and two award-winning art song cycles in association with the Limerick composer Fiona Linnane, and a new play *Diamond Rocks: Sunset*, commissioned by The Lime Tree Theatre.

MARGARET LONERGAN is a visual art practitioner who works through the disciplines of design, typography, drawing and photography depending on the moment, the call and the context. She has a long-standing commission with Imram Féile Litríochta Gaeilge to create large-scale image projections for theatre performances of poetry, prose and music in Irish, Scots Gaelic, French, German and English. She worked at the National College of Art and Design, 1991–2009, first as a lecturer in Art and Design Education, and latterly as Head of the Department of Visual Communication. www.margaretlonergan.com